I Ain't Ascared of Nutin'...
The Evolution of Me

by

Kyndall Brown

Forward by
Dad

©2007 Kyndall Amber Brown

This work is licensed under a
Creative Commons Attribution-NoDerivs 2.5 License.

Published in the United States by
Buddafly Books

ISBN: 978-0-6151-4988-2

The Evolution…

from the beginning… then to the end… and then back to the beginning…

Table of Contents

A Father's Pride.. 9
I Ain't Ascared of Nutin' 11
Why Me? 13
Nothing Can Hold Me Back 15
I Will Succeed 17
My Diary 19
What is it Like to Loose a Friend? 21
Friendship 23
When is War Going to Stop? 25
Can You Live in My Dreams? 27
I Saw What You Did 29
Butterflies 31
This Girl I Know 33
Tell It 35
What Ever Happened 37
Peace on Earth… What Does it Really Mean? 39
This is Where It Began 41
War 43
Get It Right 45
Homelessness 47
Little Sis Walked Away 49
Listen 51
Someone Stole My Friend 53
Thank you for You 55
The End 57

The Poet...

Kyndall Brown is 11 years old. She attends Anne Beers Elementary School in Washington DC. Kyndall is a member of the poetry group Girls and Boys with Hearts (GBWH). GBWH was founded and is directed by Ladi Di (the Love Poet). Kyndall also participates in DC Scores at Anne Beers. DC SCORES provides creative writing and soccer activities each day after-school. Anne Beers has won the DC Score's Poetry Slam 4 of the last 6 years. A first place prize winner of the 2005 Washington DC Poetry Fest Slam Championship, Kyndall has performed her poetry on various stages and venues in the  DC metropolitan area including the Pantene Totally You Tour at the Washington Convention Center, the DC Poetry Festival at the Carter Baron Amphitheatre and in the Langston Room at Busboys and Poets Café and Book Store. Kyndall also had a cameo appearance in the Larry Neal Award winning dramatic play "Prison Poetry" by "Papi" Kymone Freeman at the Lincoln Theater. Kyndall is active in the community. She has performed at community rallies and festivals, including the October 2006 rally to reopen the Anacostia Public Library, the Black History Poetry Festival at Iverson Mall, in Hillcrest Heights, MD and the Black LUV Festival in Washington D.C. She also makes regular appearances at the open mic event at Caravan Books in Oxon Hill MD. Her work has been published in the Beltway Poetry Quarterly (The Wartime Issue) and in ECHOES: Voices from Prince George's County Poets. Kyndall Brown has also been a featured poet on the 2KNation radio program at WPFW 89.3FM in Washington DC.

Forward

A Father's Pride..

Kyndall was never shy. She has always been the first, the last, and the most unforgettable character, speaker, dancer, athlete or poet in every event she has ever participated in. At least that's the way I remember it. You might say my judgment is clouded by a father's pride and love for his daughter. I might agree with you if her poetry wasn't so deep, so real, and so full of thought. A friend of mine once read one of her poems and after a brief moment of silence he said, "Kyndall has been here before". He further explained that her poem, "What it's Like to loose a Friend", took him back to a time when he lost his best friend. He said the only way she could have touched those places or explained those feelings was to have been there. By the way, she wrote that poem when she was nine years old. My friend... well he is "forty something" and he lost his best friend when he was a young child. Her poetry has a way of touching you like that. It moves in and around politics, religion, faith, self pride, love, pain and the realities of living in Washington DC. Her poem "I Saw What You Did" takes you to all these places and drops you off at the edge of despair in a few short verses of inner reflection. I remember someone saying that the gift of a great poet is to be able to construct poetic verses that move each reader in a unique and deeply personal way. Well... Kyndall is no Maya Angelou or Nikki Giovanni... she is only eleven as I write this forward.... but her work will move you, make you proud, make you cry, make you shout and make you want to take action. A father's pride is a wonderful thing. You remember the roses... never the thorns, the happy times never the tears. Your child is always the most excellent, never the ordinary. This book is definitely full of the extraordinary. Read it... be proud... cry about loosing your best friend... shout about the unfairness of life... and then **TAKE ACTION**.

Love Always...
Dad

Poem – 1

I Ain't Ascared of Nutin'

I ain't asared of nutin'.

Not scared to have fun.
Not ascared to jump off a hill.
Not scared to cut a dollar bill.
Not scared of you.

I ain't scared of nutin'.

Not ascared to yell.
Not ascared to call my mom.
Not ascared of that fat man.
Not ascared to do anything.
Not ascared of a monster.

Not ascared to fight for freedom.

Poem – 2

<u>Why Me?</u>

Why me?
Why am I so Late?
Why am I acting like this?

Why Me?

Where am I going?
Why is MY Head Aching?

Why ME?

What is she doing?
Where is my Mommy?
Where is my Daddy?
Where is MY School?
Where is our House?
Where am I!!!?

Why Me?

Why are my GRADES so low?
What is wrong with my TEACHER?
Where is my sister?
Where is my cat?
Where is my DOG?

Where is EVERYTHING…?

Poem – 3
(June 23, 2005)

Nothing Can Hold Me Back

Nothing can hold me back!

Because…

I have all the power, strength and faith I need.
I will succeed!!
I am an African American… and Female too.
No one can tell me I'll fail.

What makes me so confident you ask?

You see…
It's God above…
My friends and family…
And programs like Girls and Boys with Hearts…
Being my strength, hope and faith…
Teaching me to write poetry and learning about life….
Showing me how to be proud and confident…
Giving me support and all the love I need.

I will Never… Ever… Stop!

I am on my way to the top!

Nothing can hold me back!

Poem – 4

I Will Succeed

I will succeed.

I will be a character in every movie you will ever see.

I am a rare actress as you can tell.

I am Honest…

Beautiful and all about ME.

Some people may talk about me…

But I know I am the best of the best.

Try me and see… I will past any test.

I will succeed!

Oh Yes!!

I will succeed!!!

Poem – 5

My Diary

My diary tells all about me.

My diary tells all about my good days.
My diary tells all about my bad days.
My diary tells what I like.
My diary tells about what I don't like.

In my diary… there are good people.

In my diary… there are bad people.

My diary tells what happens at school…
My diary tells what happens at home…
My diary tells what happens at church…

My diary tells all about me.

Who I am?
What things I do??
What kind of person I am???

In my diary… there are dreams, hopes and prayers.

Do you have a diary?

Will your diary tell good things about you??

Poem – 6

What is it Like to Loose a Friend?

What is it like to loose a friend? Do you know?

I don't think so!

One day I asked my mother… where he was?
What was he doing?
What happened to him?
She said… He went away! He would not come back!
He Died!
Do you know what it is like to loose a friend?

I don't think so!

He died on Tuesday. How could he? Why did he?
Why would he?
I cried… and cried… and cried.
I cried so hard… my nose began to bleed.
Do you know what it is like to loose a friend?

I don't think so!

You see… I loved him. I thought he loved me too…
I said… I loved him and he loved me too…
Do you know what it is like to loose a friend?

I don't think so!

Why did he have to leave?
I'm only nine years old! Why now? Why ever?
You see… I loved that cat! I thought… He loved me too?
Do you know what it is like to loose a… pet?

Now you do! Goodbye Mr. Puddy Cat. My friend!

Poem – 7

Friendship

People are confused…
They just don't know…

What's the true meaning of friendship?

You call me your friend… and turn around and dis me.
You take from me… and give nothing at all.
You tell me you care… and tell them you don't.

You are very confused…
You just don't know…

What's the true meaning of friendship?

Let me explain…

Trust me and I'll trust you…
Respect me and I'll respect you…
Be honest with me and I'll be honest with you…
Give me your friendship and I'll give mine to you…

Friendship… do you understand?

Trust… Respect… Honesty…
That's the true meaning of friendship.

Do you have a real friend?

I do…

Poem – 8

When is War Going to Stop?

When will war end?

This war… That war…
Your war… Our war…
Does it really matter?

When is war going to stop?

Will it be today?
Will it be tomorrow, or next week?
End it now! Today!! This minute!!!

Now!!!!

If it does not stop…

Soon there will be no Teachers…
No Firefighters… No Mothers…
No Fathers… No Sisters or Brothers.

But most of all…

No America? God Bless America??

Why would He???

Poem – 9

Can You Live in My Dreams?

Can you live in my dreams?

Can you spend your entire life in my nightmares?

Can you face the monsters in my reality?

Unemployment…

Poverty…

Crime…

Homelessness…

Child Abduction…

War…

Dreams, Nightmares, Reality, is there a difference?

Can you live in my dreams?

Can you spend your entire life in my nightmares?

Can you face the monsters in my reality?

Why would anyone want to?

Poem – 10

I Saw What You Did

I saw what you did…

I saw you create jealousy, envy and greed.
I saw you destroy one of the world's oldest civilizations.
I saw you implant that jealousy, envy and greed into the hearts of the innocent.

I saw what you did…

I saw you turn brother against brother, sister against sister and friend against friend.

I saw what you did…

I saw you break their hearts.
I saw you tell jealousy and envy to kill half of them and greed to kill the rest.

I saw them die…

I saw their blood on the sidewalks and the streets.
How could you do such an evil thing?
Sometimes I don't believe… I saw what you did.

But I did… I saw you.
Yeah…

I saw what you did…

And it haunts me forever.

Poem – 11
(August 2006)

Butterflies

Butterflies…
Beautiful creations of God…
Wings of soft colors
Blue, Green, Purple and White
Transparent shadows floating through the air

Butterflies…
Flying all around me…
Their silky wings pushing them up to the sky
I can see them floating on invisible currents of air
I can almost feel them…
A beautiful breeze lightly touching the palm of my hand

Butterflies…
Butterflies…
All around me
Natures symbol of beauty.

Butterflies…
Butterflies…
All around me

Oh how I love Butterflies

Poem – 12

<u>This Girl I Know</u>

She's got so many people… pushing her… lifting her up
Yet… so many… pulling her… knocking her down
Smashing her dreams to dust

Beautiful… Intelligent… Strong… this girl I know

Ugly… Stupid… Weak they say… filling her mind with doubt
Lonely… Hopeless… Confused… she believes every word they say
Like her… so many… on the brink of self destruction… killing themselves

Beautiful… Intelligent… Strong… this girl I know

Getting high on drugs… the alcohol is the only way she feels good
Soon she's lost… out of control… no way to get back
Where should she go? What should she do? After all she's been through!

Beautiful… Intelligent… Strong… this girl I know

She's got so many people… pulling her… knocking her down
Yet… so many… pushing her… lifting her up
Up on wings of Beauty… Intelligence… and Strength

Let her fly…

Beautiful… Intelligent… Strong… this girl I know

Let her fly… Let her fly… Let her be free

Poem – 13
(10-10-2006)

Tell It

Don't be scared to speak the truth
Free your self and speak your mind

Today is the day you come out
Loose those chains… let them go… and free yourself

Tell it

You're beautiful, strong and smart
Don't let them lock you up and put chains on your heart

Ain't nothing wrong with you
Show them… Tell them… Be yourself

Today is the day they'll listen to your words
Today is the day they'll see your truth

Free yourself and speak your mind
Don't be scared to speak the truth

Tell it… Shout it… Speak it

Loose those chains and free your mind
Loose those chains and free your heart
Loose those chains and free your soul

Tell it… Shout it… Speak it

You're beautiful, strong and smart
Don't let them lock you up and put chains on your heart

Tell it

**Don't be scared to speak the truth
Free yourself and speak your mind**

**Today is the day you come out
Loose those chains… let them go… and free your soul**

Poem – 14
(10-11-2006)

What Ever Happened

What Ever Happened?

What ever happened to those days we talked about?
We talked about love…
We talked about happiness…
We talked about peace…

What Ever Happened?

What ever happened to those good people?
Their hearts are full of hate…
They live homeless in the street…
They murder and kill the babies…

What Ever Happened?

What ever happened to the promise?
You promised I would be safe.
You promised me a good education.
You promised I could be all that I imagined.

What Ever Happened?

What happened to you?
What happened to them?
What happened to us?

You… Them… Us… This!!!

This… is what happened to me.

Poem – 15
(01-06-2007)

Peace on Earth... What Does it Really Mean?

What does it really mean?
Is there really Peace on Earth?

Sure Mom says "Love thy neighbor" and "Mind your manners"
But there's stealing, fighting, and killing...
No... not just the kids I'm talking about the parents.

So why do you say... Peace on Earth.
It's clear to me...you don't see what I see...

Again you say "We're here to help" and "We'll feed the poor"
But you send soldiers, bombs and death as your ambassador

So why do you say... Peace on Earth?
It's clear to me... you don't see what I see...

In this reality... our world is filled with hate.
In this reality... our world is filled with war.
In this reality... our world is filled with poverty.

Do you know...? What does Peace on Earth really mean?
It's clear to me... you must change your philosophy...

You must... replace hate with love.
You must... replace war with peace.
You must... replace poverty with sharing.

Do you know...? What does Peace on Earth really mean?
It's clear to me... you must change your strategy...

Give love... the world will be a better place.
Stop all wars... talk through your problems.

Feed the poor… show someone you care.

Peace on Earth.
So tell me… do you really know what that means?

Please… Let there be Peace on Earth.

The Anne Beers Chapter

<u>This is Where It Began...</u>

"From the beginning... then to the end... and then back to the beginning..." I forgot who said that but Kyndall is eleven years old now and getting ready for middle school. The evolution from the beginning into the now has begun. Where have the years gone? She began writing when she was only eight years old. At the time she was attending Anne Beers Elementary School in Washington DC and participating in a unique program called DC Scores. DC SCORES brings together academics and athletics by providing students with creative writing and soccer activities each day after-school. I remember when Kyndall discovered Anne Beers had a soccer team... "Daddy... Daddy... can I play soccer? I'll do all my homework... I'll keep my room clean... I'll eat all my vegetables... Please!!! Please!!! Can I play?" Her first year on the team she played with girls twice her size... a child among giants... I thought. But they couldn't match her passion for competition... her determination to be the best. She quickly became a first team player. She approached poetry with the same passion and determination. Poetry Slam was the competition where she was determined to be triumphant. Her poem "I Ain't Ascared of Nutin'." was written as part of her first DC Scores writing assignment. The Anne Beers slam team was coached that year to a third consecutive DC Scores Poetry Slam championship. Together, the students and their coach, Ms Brock, wrote a diverse collection of thought provoking and inspiring poems that launched contemporary topics... Self Pride, Homelessness, War, and Politics... like missiles from the pages of elementary school notebooks through the voices of young poets. The Anne Beers slam team performed their poems at various venues and community events all over the Washington DC metropolitan area. The poems that follow are but a few that Kyndall and her poetry slam teammates wrote and performed while participating in DC Scores.

Love Always...
Dad

Poem – 16

<u>War</u>

Is President Bush in the house?

Are the Joint Chiefs of Staff around?

Where are the members of the house of Senate or Congress? Well that's usual when a child's got something to say those that need to hear it aren't ever around.

There is rumor of war; we heard it last night on the six o'clock news. Yet instead of countries getting together to talk and try to work things out it's fighting that they choose.

Isn't it clear that war only means a lot of people will loose their lives, their homes and peace of mind? Why hasn't someone come up with another solution?

Isn't killing a crime?

War, War, War... how can such a little word mean so much death and destruction. Grown ups use it to settle their problems..., but when children have conflicts, "don't fight is their instruction."

Bombs guns and tanks are all things that hurt.

War is a trap of Danger that leaves broken bodies in the dirt.

Don't the leaders of the world remember wars of the past... whose memory brings sadness that will forever last.

If war is the answer... then

I declare war on poverty
I declare war on drugs
I declare war on poor education
I declare war for freedom... and for that... I'd fight

I declare war on war

We need peace in the world.
We deserve the chance to live out our lives.

If war is an answer... then what was the question?

Anne Beers Elementary School
DC Scores Poetry Slam Team
Ms. Brock, Coach

Poem – 17

Get It Right

Before you say anything about me…
Get the facts… know what you are talking about.
Don't assume anything from what you see.

Get it Right

Yeah I'm African American and female too…
And every stereotype you've heard about me just ain't true.

So before you draw any conclusions or have any opinion that negatively categorizes me, getting your information straight is the thing you need to do.

Get it Right

You may be wondering what I'm really trying to say...
It's as simple as this....

I'm tired of the hype, the confusion that stands in my way. These crazy accusations about young black sisters that hinder us and cause some of us to stray…

Just Get it Right

Change all the negative things you print and say, because African American girls accomplish great things every day.

We are not plagued with unwanted pregnancies or joblessness.

We're going to college and becoming lawyers, doctors and engineers.

Yeah… and we'll be starting our own businesses.

We won't be sitting around making excuses or complaining about the economy. In every area of our lives we'll have victory... You watch and see.

Take a good long look and recognize the future. Young black girls like me standing ready all over the world. You should be helping, motivating, and encouraging them.

Get it Right...

Anne Beers Elementary School
DC Scores Poetry Slam Team
Ms. Brock, Coach

Poem – 18

Homelessness

Where are you going to go tonight after the show?
When you are tired and sleepy... Where will you go?
To a bridge or a park bench... a subway grates...
No... I don't think so.

If you are lucky you are going home... to a house, trailer or an apartment.

You won't have to sleep out on the cold cement.
You have a place to eat and watch TV.
You can take a warm bath.
And you have a cozy bed to sleep in.

I don't... Yeah you heard right I don't.
For I am homeless you see.
Home for me is where ever I happen to be.

I guess you can't tell
I look normal enough
My clothes are clean and my hair is neat.
And I don't look like I need food to eat.
But you better believe I don't have anywhere to sleep

There is so much going on in our city these days

Extra!!! Extra!!! Read all about it...

The schools' Superintendent Quit...
Metro plans to go up another 50 cents...
The Redskins loose again...
School violence never ends.

These are all major events... but we never hear about Homelessness...

Everyone deserves a place to live… I know I do

I'd like a roof over my head at night too

The next time you see some homeless person
Don't laugh or ignore them… It might be me

And if times get hard enough It might be you.

Anne Beers Elementary School
DC Scores Poetry Slam Team
Ms. Brock, Coach

Poem – 19

Little Sis Walked Away

I only looked away for a moment.

She was right here holding my hand.
We were standing in the spot we always do.
Between the bus stop and the news stand.

I am careful, I promise, but in an instant she was gone.
My baby sister was standing in the middle of the street.
I screamed her name.

Jamie, Jamie…

But through the sound of traffic she couldn't hear.
She stood there frozen, trembling with fear.

I love my sister though; I am mean to her sometimes.
She's a baby and I get mad at her when tattles and whines.
She's always under my feet but she's very dear to my heart.
She's my baby sister and we should never be apart.

Suddenly a car
Fast and loud, red and black
I reached out and yelled

Jamieeeeeeeeee…………

Come back

Anne Beers Elementary School
DC Scores Poetry Slam Team
Ms. Brock, Coach

Poem – 20

Listen

Listen, Listen, Listen to us and hear what we have to say.
It might not seem important to you but listen anyway.

My view point is different from those you may have heard
before. What I have to say is something you shouldn't ignore.

I've seen things and experienced a lot too. What I have
learned could help and encourage you.

Listen and you might find out why I won't listen to you.
Listen and our relationship might grow stronger and we
might get closer too.

Did you ever wonder why you really don't know me?
Could it be possible that it's because you never listen to me.

Listen, I 'm trying to make it clear so that you can see…
You'll find out who I am if you just listen to me.

After all I've said, you're still not listening now.
Your eyes should be on me, I don't want to hear a sound.
I said I've got something important to say.

Whatever; forget it you won't listen anyway…

Anne Beers Elementary School
DC Scores Poetry Slam Team
Ms. Brock, Coach

Poem – 21

Someone Stole My Friend

(In loving memory of All Missing children)

Somebody took our friend.
They stole her from her home.
We went to her house today to play and the police said, "She was gone"

"Who would do such a thing? Why?
It's mean to make someone's mommy and Daddy cry.
I heard her mommy whisper to God "Don't let my baby die"

You hear on the news about missing children, abused children, and neglected children murdered children their futures snatched away.

We never thought, or even imagined this would happen to us here in our neighborhood. We'd do anything to get our friend back if we could.

Our whole community is torn apart, families are shaken and in shock.

There is no laughter or children playing just policeman hanging around our block.

Parents and Teachers always say, "That there are mean people in the world who want to hurt children like you and me.
We're just little kids just trying to understand life, why don't they just let us is.

Aren't we the future, precious in God's sight?
We shouldn't have to worry about our safety during the day or night.

Someone should be looking out for us and protecting us and
keeping us out of harms way.
We want to grow up, live productive lives but. most
importantly we want to be worry free when we go out to play

Does anybody care?
Our friend was stolen, taken away
Is anyone listening out there?

Anne Beers Elementary School
DC Scores Poetry Slam Team
Ms. Brock, Coach

Thanks to You
(March 2006)

Thank you for You

Thank you Sylvia Dianne Beverly (Ladi Di). Thank you for you. I met Ladi Di when I was in third grade. She helped me find my poetic voice. She taught me how to write poetry and how to feel what you write. She has helped form my poetry into a unique expression of me. I can never thank her enough. She opened so many doors and opportunities. Without her I would not be in this place… all these people… all these places… Thank you Ladi Di… You have done so much for me.

Thank you (Papi) Kymone Freeman. Thank you for you. I met Mr. Freeman at my first poetry event. The event was hosted by Ladi Di. It was a Black History Month poetry festival and there was a stage, a mic and people from all around the Washington DC area. I didn't think anyone would want to hear what I had to say. Mr. Freeman sat next to me and noticed the poem I had in my hands. He read "I Ain't Ascared of Nutin" and liked it… That day he taught me to be comfortable with what I had to say… Thanks Mr. Freeman for helping me and providing me with many, many opportunities to write what I feel and speak what I write. Thank you for everything you have done for me.

Thank you Ms. Brock. Thank you for you. Ms. Brock is our DC Scores poetry coach at Anne Beers. They told me she was tough. They told me she would yell… they told me she would make you practice over and over… They didn't tell me how much she would love all of us. Ms. Brock helped me overcome stage fright. She showed me how to perform with excitement. She gave each and everyone of us a piece of her own passion. Every time we walked on stage we knew she was there with us… Thank you Ms. Brock so much for everything you have done for me.

Thank you all for you. Thank you Mommy, Daddy, family, Anne Beers Elementary School and my closest friends… but most of all thank you God. I've been truly blessed.

The End

The End

Is this the end???

Just for now… more to come for sure…

"From the beginning… then to the end… and then back to the beginning…" I forgot who said that but the evolution of Kyndall Brown has just begun.

I can't wait for the next part of the journey…

Love Always…
Dad

**Anne Beers Elementary School
2006 DC Scores Poetry Slam**
(Kyndall Brown at the microphone)
Photograph by Paul Morigi
http://www.prmorigi.com

www.ingramcontent.com/pod-product-compliance
Lightning Source LLC
Chambersburg PA
CBHW031428040426
42444CB00006B/730